SPRINTING THROUGH SETBACKS

This journal belongs to:

If found:

Journaling has always been my secret weapon in my career as a 400-meter runner. Even back in college, if I wasn't running, I was probably journaling about it, using writing as a way to figure out what I needed to work on, how I could improve, and so much more.

After 2020—a tough year for all of us—I knew running consistently was what I struggled to do, so I started journaling on how I could be more consistent if I had any hope of making my next team. I started writing about how I needed to believe in myself at every single practice and to be intentional every time I showed up to the track. Teaching myself consistency would mean that I couldn't phone anything in. Everything needed to be dialed. Consistent and committed had to become my watch words for the year, in every area of my life. It worked.

Similarly, my race day routine has been honed over the years—and journaling is a key part of that. I lay out my clothes the day before the race, especially if I'm sharing a hotel room since you don't want to be a bad roommate digging for your stuff early in the morning. What I'm going to wear depends on the race, so I make sure that I have the right clothing laid out. My competition clothing is different from what I wear in most practices, but I love that because it's a little sign to my brain when I put those clothes on that it's time to get serious. When that kit goes on, it's the 'real effort' day. But more importantly, I also spend some time with my journal, going over the plan for the next day, writing out my race intentions.

step into your spotlight

What does the idea of *spotlight* mean to you?

At first, I worried that writing out intentions for a race would make me stressed out and I'd get stuck in my own head. But in reality, I just needed to rethink how I was forming my intentions. Yes, times matter, but in races, setting a time goal isn't really enough—you need more of a 'how' to go with the 'what.' So I started making intentions for races like getting out really strong on the first 100, staying in contact with at least one other runner who started in front of me, or coming into the last 100 really pumping my arms. Details that I could focus on that would get me to my time goal.

This isn't manifesting. It's not like you just close your eyes and if you believe it enough, you'll run fast. Instead, you write down 'get out strong' as your intention for your workouts, practice that often enough that it comes naturally when you're writing it down and heading to the track on race day. Your body gets used to it, because you've practiced. And you've been able to practice it and embody it fully because you've journaled on it over and over. By the time you're in a race, you're ready to be consistent. You have a strong start, because that's what you've practiced. You stay in contact with the girl who was in the lane next to you, and you're aware of what's happening around you while still focusing on your own race. And you come into the finish pumping your arms and pushing as hard as you can. That's how you create consistency—and it almost always translates into a good time.

Here, I'm sharing prompts based on the chapters in my book, *Sprinting Through Setbacks*. Whether you've read the book or not (though I hope you have!), these prompts and journal pages will help you get clear on your goals, dial in your routines, hone your style, and kick negative self-talk and imposter syndrome to the curb. Grab a pen, get cozy, and let's get to work!

-Micha Powell

sprinting through setbacks

WHAT LEGACY (OR LEGACIES) DO YOU WANT TO LEAVE BEHIND?

So much of my story is about the desire to create legacies for myself, and I think that's something everyone wants! Think about this in a few ways: Try 1 year, 5 years and then, your whole life legacy. This helps bring it a little bit closer to the present day and feel more achievable rather than some esoteric exercise you'll do once and forget about!

My 1 year legacy will be... _____
(Ex: Setting the school record)

3 ways you're working towards this:

1: _____
2: _____
3: _____

My 5 year legacy will be... _____
(Ex: Going to the Olympics)

3 ways you're working towards this:

1: _____
2: _____
3: _____

My lifelong legacy will be... _____
(Ex: Being known as a record-breaking runner who also gave back to her community every year of her life.)

3 ways you're working towards this:

1: _____
2: _____
3: _____

sprinting through setbacks

CAN YOU USE COMPARISON OR ENVY AS A MOTIVATOR?

A big hurdle for me is comparing myself to my Olympian parents, but everyone has people they compare themselves to or envy. Maybe there's someone on social media who you constantly compare yourself to, or maybe it's someone in your class. Comparison and envy can be bad, *if* you let them turn your thinking negative. But you can use the feelings of comparison and envy as information and motivation. I've always tried to see my parents' successes as motivators for my own... It's not always easy, but it's worth it!

Make a list of a few people you often compare yourself to or wish you had their life.

From that list, write down what about those people makes you compare yourself to them. What do you wish you have that they have?
(Sometimes making this list actually shows you that you don't *really* want their life, you just like how it looks on Instagram... but sometimes it actually helps you see what goals really matter to you!)

Now that you know what exactly you're envious of or comparing yourself to, you can make a plan to work towards achieving that goal for yourself!

sprinting through setbacks

SETTING YOURSELF UP FOR SUCCESS

Getting the school record in the 400-meter really began in my junior year of high school, the day I was at the track in Toronto and introduced myself to the coach from the University of Maryland. If I hadn't gone up and started a conversation, *maybe* he would have noticed my running ability, but he may not have been as interested in bringing me onto the team a year later. Now, whenever I'm in a new situation, I try to introduce myself to the people around me and have real conversations, because you never know what could come from that.

It's such a superpower to think, 'How am I going to take up space in this room? How am I going to put myself in the best possible situation?' This is true for athletics, it's true for friendships and relationships, it's true for school and work. Even if you're a naturally shy person, you can still show up and own a room.

Write a list of people you'd love to interact with more than you currently do. How can you start more meaningful conversations with them?

What are some conversation starters that you can remember for when you do meet new people?

Is there a mantra or even something you can do physically to get yourself in the 'I got this' mindset when meeting new people?
(Examples: Standing up straight, counting to five in your head, telling yourself 'I've got this')

be a beginner

Where do you feel like a beginner in your life?

sprinting through setbacks

MOVE THROUGH EMBARRASSING MOMENTS

Move through embarrassing moments with grace—and get smarter along the way! We often build these awkward moments up in our minds as huge life-changing things, but if you get honest about it, you often realize that it wasn't as bad as you thought.

What's one embarrassing moment that you can look back on now and reframe into a lesson you learned?

Looking back at that embarrassing moment (since we're there anyway!)... In hindsight, does it matter at all? Did it change your life? If you asked people who were there about it, would anyone even remember?

What about a tiny embarrassing moment you've had or a little mistake you made recently? How can you grow from that small moment? (Growth doesn't just happen with big things!)

sprinting through setbacks

CREATE A 'LET IT GO' RITUAL

The next time an embarrassing moment happens (and it will!) or you make a mistake, what's a little ritual or routine that you can do to move past it? Maybe it's dancing to a certain song, maybe you vow to take five minutes to journal on it in your Notes app, maybe you just plan to text a good friend with a certain emoji so they know to say something nice. Having this ready will make the next not-so-great moment much easier to move through.

LET IT GO RITUAL #1

LET IT GO RITUAL #2

WHAT SONGS WILL HELP?

WHO CAN YOU CALL?

sprinting through setbacks

DECIDE NOW HOW YOU WANT TO BE KNOWN LATER

What impact do you want to have on people? How do you want people to feel after an interaction with you?

_____
_____
_____
_____

How would you like to be described by someone who knows you? (This can be a sentence or just a few words that you hope would describe you.)

_____
_____
_____
_____
_____
_____

Go beyond that... What do you want to be known for in terms of achieving your goals? (This can be things like 'she always gets things done on time' or 'she's a fierce competitor.' These may not be the first things that come to mind for how you want to be described as a person—this is about your goal achievement and work ethic!)

_____
_____
_____
_____
_____
_____
_____
_____

sprinting through setbacks

DECIDE NOW HOW YOU WANT TO BE KNOWN

Sum it up: What are the 3-5 words you want to describe yourself with, after doing those exercises? Are there ways you can lean into those words a little more? Write the words and then journal on how you can embody them.

_____
_____
_____
_____
_____
_____
_____
_____
_____
_____
_____
_____
_____
_____
_____
_____
_____
_____
_____
_____

Bonus points: Actually bring a friend or two into this exercise and ask them to write down a few words or sentences that describe you, and do the same for them. Check what they said versus how you want to be seen. If the two don't match, that's not a bad thing—it's just something to think about! (For example, in high school I definitely would have said that I was someone who always did her own thing, but looking back, I bet my friends actually would have described me as someone who got along with everyone and worked hard to fit in! That information would have been great, because it would have reminded me to be more of an individual and to be proud of that.)

Where in your life do you need to SHOW UP?
Races, school presentations, work meetings...
Where do you need to be ready to win?

find your calm

sprinting through setbacks

FIND YOUR POWER-UP

If someone says something discouraging to you, how do you turn that into ammunition rather than letting it get you down? This could mean creating a 'reset' plan—repeating a mantra five times, listening to a certain pump-up song, anything that can get you back into the zone!

Write down an example of when you might need this power-up and how you want to feel:

My mantra:

My pump-up music:

sprinting through setbacks

PREP FOR THE WORST CASE

If you tend to be someone who gets stressed out before big events because you're thinking about everything that can go wrong, try this exercise: Imagine a big event, whether it's a school project, job interview, race or competition.

Now, picture a few 'worst case scenarios.' Think of things that *might* go wrong that are stressing you out. After you've made that list, go back and for each scenario, write out exactly how you could handle it to take control of the situation.

This way, you're prepared for some of the things that might go wrong, but more importantly, you've shown yourself that even in worst case scenarios, there are ways to get through them! Doing this for any situation that has you stressed helps you become more adaptable and resilient, because it helps build that problem-solving mindset and muscle.

Worst case scenario #1:
I can troubleshoot/control this situation by:

Worst case scenario #2:
I can troubleshoot/control this situation by:

Worst case scenario #3:
I can troubleshoot/control this situation by:

Worst case scenario #4:
I can troubleshoot/control this situation by:

Worst case scenario #5:
I can troubleshoot/control this situation by:

sprinting through setbacks

LEARN TO SAVOR YOUR VICTORIES

Ask yourself: How do you celebrate your victories? If you're like me, you likely end up going instantly on to the next thing rather than savoring the moment. But you deserve a celebration when you have a great race, nail the presentation, or get the job. So right now, let's brainstorm a few different ways to celebrate—at different price points, for different levels of 'hooray!' moments.

Free to $5
(ex: a spa night at home giving yourself a manicure and watching a cheesy movie)

Option 1:

Option 2:

Option 3:

$10-$30
(ex: picking up your favorite takeout on the way home)

Option 1:

Option 2:

Option 3:

$50+
(ex: dinner at a fancy restaurant, taking the whole team out for ice cream, actually going to get a facial, manicure or salon visit)

Option 1:

Option 2:

Option 3:

sprinting through setbacks

THINK AHEAD TO WHAT MIGHT BE NEXT

My record-setting Olympic standard result at Regionals in 2016 kicked off a whirlwind that didn't end until I was back in school the next fall after going to the Olympics. I had no idea it was going to be as hectic as it was, but in hindsight, I could have seen it coming and been more prepared for it. The same thing happens when you get accepted to a college or you get the job after a terrifying interview: so often, we see the end goal as getting the job or hitting that one result, and we forget to look a little further ahead.

So, look at a couple of your current goals in your life. What would it look like if you *did* accomplish them? What could happen when you hit them? What might be next? Is there anything you should be preparing for now? You might be surprised at how thinking about what could be next leads you to dream bigger and close in on those current goals even faster.

_____
_____
_____
_____
_____
_____
_____
_____
_____
_____
_____
_____
_____
_____
_____
_____
_____

Where in your life do you find yourself shrinking down?

sprinting through setbacks

IDENTIFY IMPOSTER SYNDROME IN YOUR LIFE

Most of us have experienced Imposter Syndrome at some point in our lives—it's almost unavoidable! Can you think of times where you felt like you were completely in over your head and faking it? **Make a list!**
(Ex: A school presentation, the start line at a race, or starting a new internship)

_____
_____
_____
_____
_____
_____
_____
_____
_____
_____
_____
_____
_____
_____
_____
_____
_____
_____
_____
_____
_____
_____
_____

sprinting through setbacks

GET RATIONAL ABOUT WHAT YOU ARE CAPABLE OF

From that list you just wrote, pick a couple examples that you wrote down. In the first column below, write down those examples. In the next column, for each example, write another sentence or two about *why* you felt like an imposter. What about the situation made you feel like you weren't ready, or were faking it? And finally, in the third column, write down why that feeling *isn't* accurate—or what you could do to make sure it isn't accurate in the future!

For example, if your Imposter Syndrome came before doing a presentation to your class because you felt like you weren't a good speaker... Are there examples of times where you have given a good presentation? Or are there things you could have done, like practicing your presentation with some friends, that would have helped make you feel prepared?

This is a great exercise to show you that when you actually calm down and think critically about your Imposter Syndrome, it's either inaccurate *or* it's providing some information you can work with so you're ready for next time.

IMPOSTER SYNDROME MOMENT	WHY YOU FEEL LIKE AN IMPOSTER	WHY THAT'S WRONG and/or HOW YOU CAN SHIFT YOUR MINDSET

sprinting through setbacks

NAME YOUR IMPOSTER SYNDROME

Imposter Syndrome shows up as a voice in your head telling you that you're not worthy. Rather than thinking of it as part of you, why not give her a name? I like to look at Imposter Syndrome as an annoying old friend who occasionally shows up at my door and won't stop ringing the doorbell. Having her be her own separate entity helps me see those negative thoughts for what they are—thoughts that don't serve me, that aren't representative of who I truly am.

Give your Imposter Syndrome a name here—and draw a picture or write a description of who your Imposter Syndrome is. The more you can see it as a separate entity (whether it's a snake with spectacles or a grumpy octopus or your mean first grade teacher), the easier it is to separate yourself from it.

sprinting through setbacks

START YOUR DAY RIGHT

So many of us wake up and scroll through our phones immediately, and doing that, we're instantly comparing ourselves to other people and often end up feeling less-than because of it. Here's a new challenge: Every morning, first thing when you get up, write down one thing you're proud of. It can be the tiniest accomplishment ever, or something really big. It could have happened yesterday or last year.

Starting a morning 'accomplishment list' will help you see just how much progress you actually make in a week, a month or a year! (Bonus points if you can come up with more than one thing each morning, but starting with one is a great spot.)

TODAY I'M PROUD OF...
....
....
....

TODAY I'M PROUD OF...
....
....
....

TODAY I'M PROUD OF...
....
....
....

TODAY I'M PROUD OF...
....
....
....

TODAY I'M PROUD OF...
....
....
....

TODAY I'M PROUD OF...
....
....
....

sprinting through setbacks

CREATE A POSITIVE AFFIRMATION TOOLKIT

On your phone, cultivate a Positive Affirmation Toolkit that reminds you of who you want to be, what you want to do, and the greatness that is you. I have a favorites folder with things like a video of my best race ever and pictures of me with my Olympic ring and different medals I've won. I also have a note in my Notes app that has some positive affirmations and goals for myself, plus a 'positive vibes' playlist I can turn on when I need the extra pick-me-up. Build the toolkit when you're in a good mood, and it'll help you in those tough moments. Having those videos and photos, that accomplishment list, those notes to yourself... Those can help stop Imposter Syndrome in its tracks!

sprinting through setbacks

CHOOSE "I GET TO" VERSUS "I HAVE TO"

Imposter syndrome can show up as the feeling that you are stuck doing something... even when it's something that you used to love doing! In high school, I loved how running felt. I just loved the racing and the going to meets, regardless of how I performed. Now that I'm older, it's easy to feel negative about a training day that wasn't perfect. But when I reframe it and remind myself that I get to do this as a career, it helps me see an imperfect practice as an opportunity for growth, not a problem.

Try it here! Write it out, then cross out your HAVE TO statement and recopy into GET TO.

I have to.... _____
I GET to.... _____

I have to.... _____
I GET to.... _____

I have to.... _____
I GET to.... _____

I have to.... _____
I GET to.... _____

I have to.... _____
I GET to.... _____

I have to.... _____
I GET to.... _____

embrace consistency

What habits do you currently have that you're super proud of?

sprinting through setbacks

WRITE FUTURE YOU A LOVE LETTER

Write yourself a note for you to read before taking on a tough task, whether it's a test or a race. I like doing this a few days before an event, including some motivational notes and quotes along with my goals that I've set for the day. (Take a photo of this page with your phone and save this letter to your favorites so you always have it on hand!)

sprinting through setbacks

CREATE YOUR "RACE DAY SCHEDULE" FOR WHATEVER YOU'RE DOING!

I spend a lot of time racing, so every time I have a race, I make sure my plan is written out and dialed in. What do you do normally? This could be work, school or racing. Take some time to write out every aspect of your ideal race/school/work day and the schedule that you follow, from wake up to bedtime. Get granular—writing this out helps you create smart routines and follow through with them because you can see the benefits you'll get when you do!

Time	
6 AM	
7 AM	
8 AM	
9 AM	
10 AM	
11 AM	
12 PM	
1 PM	
2 PM	
3 PM	
4 PM	
5 PM	
6 PM	
7 PM	
8 PM	
9 PM	
10 PM	

NOTES

STUFF I NEED

sprinting through setbacks

SET A REMINDER

It's really important to take some time to write down thoughts after a big event. Make a reminder on your phone for after that race, presentation or test to just jot down a few notes about how it went. I like to make a few notes about what went well first, then add a few things that I want to work on for next time. Definitely prioritize getting some positives in there: It's tempting to go a little negative and list out every single thing that went wrong, but what went right is just as important!

You can try it here, or just create a note on your phone:

What went well?

What can you improve on?

What can you try next time?

sprinting through setbacks

START TRACKING HABITS

I knew running consistently was what I struggled to do, so I started journaling on how I could be more consistent if I had any hope of making my next Olympic team. I started writing about how I needed to believe in myself at every single practice and to be intentional every time I showed up to the track. Teaching myself consistency would mean that I couldn't phone anything in. Everything needed to be dialed. Consistent and committed had to become my watch words for the year, in every area of my life.

And it wasn't just my internal dialogue that needed work. I needed to sleep more and be more careful about my bedtime. I needed to prioritize drinking electrolytes and a protein shake after every session at the gym or on the track. And on the track, every workout needed to be done with absolute dedication and intention. I needed to start fighting to hit the low end of my time ranges in intervals. This sounds a little weird, but if you do a track workout, you usually have a distance, like 200 meters, and a time range for how fast you'll run it, like 28 to 32 seconds. In the past, I may not have stressed about finishing each rep around 32 seconds. But now? Aiming for 28 became the new goal. Consistency became about consistently pushing for the better result, reaching a little bit higher every time.

On the next pages, I've included a habit tracker for you to try—or you can download a number of free habit tracking apps on your phone. Pick a couple of new habits like hydrating throughout the day or sticking to a certain bedtime that you can test out. Whatever works to keep you consistent and chasing your big goals!

HABIT TRACKER

Write down the habit you want to start doing, specific details about how you'll do it, and why it's important to your goals to get this habit right. Every day you make it happen, color in the day. The goal is to not break the chain—but don't panic if you miss a day, just get back to it tomorrow!!

(HABIT)

_____

_____

_____

_____

MO TU WE TH FR SA SU
☐ ☐ ☐ ☐ ☐ ☐ ☐
☐ ☐ ☐ ☐ ☐ ☐ ☐
☐ ☐ ☐ ☐ ☐ ☐ ☐
☐ ☐ ☐ ☐ ☐ ☐ ☐

(HABIT)

_____

_____

_____

_____

MO TU WE TH FR SA SU
☐ ☐ ☐ ☐ ☐ ☐ ☐
☐ ☐ ☐ ☐ ☐ ☐ ☐
☐ ☐ ☐ ☐ ☐ ☐ ☐
☐ ☐ ☐ ☐ ☐ ☐ ☐

(HABIT)

_____

_____

_____

_____

MO TU WE TH FR SA SU
☐ ☐ ☐ ☐ ☐ ☐ ☐
☐ ☐ ☐ ☐ ☐ ☐ ☐
☐ ☐ ☐ ☐ ☐ ☐ ☐
☐ ☐ ☐ ☐ ☐ ☐ ☐

(HABIT)

_____

_____

_____

_____

MO TU WE TH FR SA SU
☐ ☐ ☐ ☐ ☐ ☐ ☐
☐ ☐ ☐ ☐ ☐ ☐ ☐
☐ ☐ ☐ ☐ ☐ ☐ ☐
☐ ☐ ☐ ☐ ☐ ☐ ☐

HABIT TRACKER

HABIT

MO TU WE TH FR SA SU

HABIT

MO TU WE TH FR SA SU

HABIT

MO TU WE TH FR SA SU

HABIT

MO TU WE TH FR SA SU

Trust yourself + the process

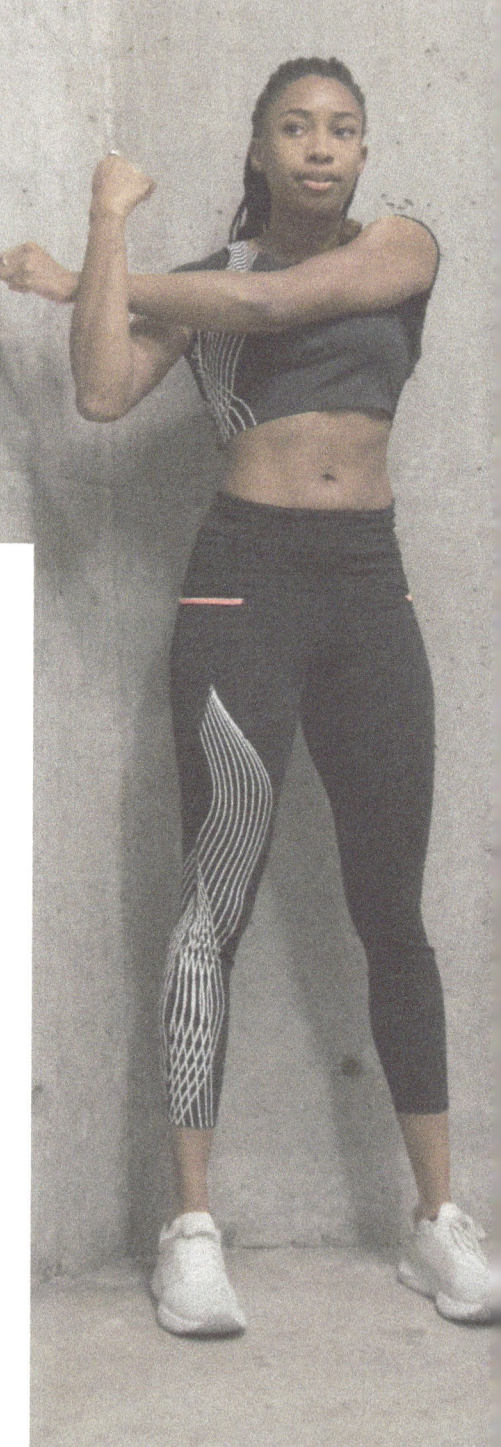

When was the last time you really listened to your body? Tune in: What is it saying?

sprinting through setbacks

HOW CAN YOU BE FULLY PREPARED?

My best races happen when I've spent a lot much time preparing and visualizing and getting ready to try something new.

When was a time you prepared really well for a test, a meet, a competition, or a presentation?

What did you do that made your preparation so good?

How can you do that same kind of preparation in other aspects of your life?

How can you set yourself up for success for an upcoming presentation or meet?

sprinting through setbacks

HOW DO YOU KNOW WHO TO TRUST?

In the TRUST chapter in my book, I talk a lot about learning when to push back against what my coach was saying, but also when to listen to him knowing that he has my best interests at heart, even when I disagree with him. That's not always easy to do! You probably have a coach or teacher or parent in your life who you don't always see eye to eye with.

When these situations come up, I try to ask myself a few questions to get clarity:

Have I made my stance clear? (In my case, that was carefully explaining exactly how my injury was progressing and how running was making my leg feel.)

Have I had an honest dialogue about it with the person? Have I very clearly stated what I feel is right for me and what my solution to the situation would be? I've realized sometimes when I was trying to tell my coach something about how I was feeling, I wasn't really expressing how I wanted to fix the situation, I was just telling him what was wrong.

If I'm still not in agreement, is there some neutral third party I can go to for an opinion? (This could be the school nurse, a guidance counselor, another teacher, a parent, or a doctor.)

Has my coach/teacher/parent been right in the past? Are they usually correct in their assessments and it's only afterwards that I (painfully) admit that they were right? (This may not inform this situation exactly, but it could help you see that they might have a point.)

Of course, it's also important to note that if you feel uncomfortable or like you're in any physical or emotional danger, you should immediately seek help from a trusted adult!

sprinting through setbacks

TEST YOUR CONSPIRACY THEORY

If you've done all of that work and still feel like you and your coach/teacher/boss/parent aren't seeing eye-to-eye, test out the Conspiracy Theory. Write out what exactly that person is trying to do to you, what their ulterior motive is. For me, that would have looked like "My coach is trying to sabotage my training by having me run while injured so I can't make the Olympic team." Writing that out and reading it makes me immediately see just how ridiculous that idea is—but deep down, that's what was going through my brain!

The key is writing it down on paper. Don't just think through this exercise, actually handwrite it and look at it. As soon as I see my conspiracy theory in writing, I instantly realize that I'm being silly. Of course my coach isn't out to get me, and it's easy for me to see that he's just acting in the way he thinks is best for me. Knowing that makes it a lot easier to come to a win-win situation. (PS: This also works for when you're in a fight or disagreement with a friend!)

WRITE YOUR CONSPIRACY THEORY HERE:

sprinting through setbacks

ASK YOURSELF: "I'M RIGHT, NOW WHAT?"

Bookmark this question for when you do win an argument with your coach/parent/teacher/friend: It's not always ideal to be proven right (like in my case, where I did have an injury but my coach wasn't listening to me).

So, if you are right in the argument, what is your next step going to be? This keeps you focused on moving forward, not just winning an argument.

I'm right, now what...

_____
_____
_____
_____
_____
_____
_____
_____
_____
_____
_____
_____
_____
_____
_____
_____
_____
_____
_____
_____

Do you feel like you're balanced with your life right now? Are you getting after that big goal?

balance your life + your goals

sprinting through setbacks

GET CLEAR ABOUT YOUR GOALS

Let's start with a few questions to help you hone on what your actual goals are!

What is your top priority in your life right now? (And yes, of course you'll want to write down more than one... but try to keep it to three, maximum.)

How much time are you giving your main priority? Is it enough or are you constantly feeling like you want to do more but are just too busy?

In an ideal week, how would you be going after your goal? What can you add that would be helpful? (For a track runner, adding extra recovery sessions might be a great one that's often ignored!)

sprinting through setbacks

GET HONEST ABOUT YOUR CURRENT SCHEDULE

Look at your last couple weeks on your calendar:
- Are you actually giving your main goals as much time as you think? Or are there other things that keep getting in the way?
- When you write out your daily schedule or to-do list, can you actually get it all done?
- Are there any things you're doing regularly that you could easily drop off of your schedule that would allow you more time and energy to focus on your main goal? (Obviously things like homework or a job you need in order to pay rent aren't going to be negotiable, but maybe it's time to give up that spot on student council if you really want to be focused on your volunteer work!)
- Where are you holding onto a resentment or a lack of confidence that could actually be holding you back instead of helping you? Is someone making you feel like you 'have' to be doing something? If so, do they honestly feel that way, or are you just projecting? (This is especially true with parents—we think they want us doing a million things, but most of the time, it's in our heads... see the last prompt about Conspiracy Theories!)

What did you find looking at your calendar?

_____
_____
_____
_____
_____
_____
_____
_____
_____
_____
_____
_____
_____
_____
_____
_____
_____
_____

sprinting through setbacks

WRITE OUT AN IDEAL SCHEDULE
BASED ON YOUR GOALS AND CURRENT LIFE

Whether you use a paper planner or a digital one, take some time to draft a new weekly schedule that leaves you time to focus on your goals, without neglecting or ignoring the other 'must do' pieces of your life. While you won't be able to hit this schedule every week, having it to refer back to is a good reminder of how you can make space for your goals.

Use this page to make notes + plan out your ideal schedule before turning the page and using the templates to make an ideal daily and weekly schedule... don't be afraid to get messy!

WEEKLY PLANNER

FROM: / / TO: / /

MON

TUE

WED

THUR

FRI

SAT

SUN

GOAL OF THE WEEK

TOP PRIORITIES

DEADLINES

TO DO LIST

Daily Planner

Date : _____

S M T W T F S

Today's Goal
☐ _____
☐ _____
☐ _____

Priority List
☐ _____
☐ _____
☐ _____

Meal Plans:

Today's Schedule
_____
07.00
_____
08.00
_____
09.00
_____
10.00
_____
11.00
_____
12.00
_____
1.00
_____
2.00
_____
3.00
_____
4.00
_____
5.00
_____
6.00
_____
7.00
_____
8.00
_____

What I need to bring with me:

Notes:

5 4 3

find your crew

Where do you feel most like you belong?

sprinting through setbacks

DEFINE BELONGING FOR YOU

What does belonging mean to you?

When have you felt like you have/haven't belonged?

What would belonging look like, if you don't currently feel like you're part of something?

What are the internal / external markers you associate with belonging?

What can you control about feeling like you belong?

What can't you control—and how can you let go of that?
(And remember, it's normal to feel like you don't belong at different points in your life! We can work on it—but it's not the end of the world!)

sprinting through setbacks

THINK ABOUT YOUR CURRENT CREW

Remember, people don't need to be chasing the same goals as you to align with your values. You might be trying to achieve greatness on the track while your bestie runs for student body president. But you both love focusing on getting the best out of yourselves and the people around you. Yes, on paper your goals are different... But your values are the same.

What are your top values?

Who are your five people you spend the most time with?

Do you feel like the people you hang out with share those values? Are they people who align with you achieving your goals? (If not, this doesn't mean ditching your current friend group—but it might mean branching out and meeting some new people!)

Are you bringing your best to your group? If not, how can you start?

sprinting through setbacks

CHOOSE YOUR INNER CIRCLE

Who's your "team"? If you don't have an actual team, who are your friends/family/coach/teachers etc. who make you feel the most capable of achieving your goals?

When was the last time you communicated your goals to them? If it's been a while, it might be time for a goal refresh session! (Make a few notes here about who you need to call!)

When was the last time you said no to something? How did it feel?

the power of 'NO'

sprinting through setbacks

FIND THE POSITIVE IN SAYING NO

Look for times in your life where saying no has worked out for you. Make a list!

_____
_____
_____
_____
_____
_____
_____
_____
_____
_____
_____
_____
_____
_____
_____
_____
_____
_____
_____
_____

sprinting through setbacks

PRACTICE YOUR NO

A lot of us struggle to say no. Consider this your chance to practice!

Write down a few common things you get asked to do that you'd rather say no to (like another horror movie marathon with a friend when you *hate* horror movies!).

How do you normally respond to those situations? Look through emails and texts to see how you've responded in the past. Are you way too apologetic when you say no? Do you say yes in the moment but get grumpy about it later?

What are three ways you could say no instead? I love an unapologetic 'no' that also offers the option you're willing to do. For example, I was feeling under the weather because I had a hectic week. I texted my coach, "Hey, Coach, I'm taking Monday off because I don't feel great. I'm going to use the extra day to relax and recover. I'll see you Tuesday." I wasn't apologizing, I didn't offer a big explanation—I was just clear about saying no to practice on Monday, and gave him my solution, which was to shift practice to Tuesday instead.

sprinting through setbacks

FIND YOUR ACCIDENTAL "YES" TRIGGERS

What triggers bring on the feelings of having to do something, or say yes to something you'd rather not do? Has that led to bad outcomes? How does it feel in those moments in your body? Do you get sweaty? Does your heart rate increase?

Be ready to take a step back - what are basic questions you can ask yourself to bring you back into the moment? Write them down so you remember them. (Questions like 'how do I actually feel?' or 'do I have time in my schedule for that?' are great options since they force you to step back and objectively survey the scene.)

What's a simple mantra/reminder to remember for these moments? (Something simple that's easy to remember like 'pause' is a great one!)

sprinting through setbacks

DEFINE FUTURE YOU

When I make decisions now, I'm thinking about how they will impact Future Micha. Am I making the best choice for the person I want to be? Having a vision of Future Micha helps me make the best possible decisions for me now and me in the future.

Who is Future You? Describe her! Get as detailed as you want, and go as far into the future as you want. Maybe Future You is just a year from now, maybe she's 10 years older. Find what feels right for you! Write about her, draw her out—paint yourself a picture!

Once you define your Future You, keep a few notes about her somewhere you see regularly, like your mirror in the bathroom, your locker or your journal. Whenever you're making decisions, try to bring Future You to mind: What would she say or do?

define your style

What does the word *style* mean to you?

sprinting through setbacks

DEFINE YOUR IDEAL STYLE

What do you want your style to say about you? (You may want to think about this by asking how you would want someone else to describe your style.)

What pieces/styling elements make you feel most you?

What words, moods, music, or colors signify the 'you' that you want the world to know?

What is your OUTFIT?
You know—the one that makes you feel like you can do anything! (For me, this is my orange one-piece for racing.) You might have a couple for different aspects of your life, like one that makes you feel like a boss for a school presentation versus your race day outfit. But you may notice some similarities between the two in terms of colors and style!

INSPIRATION

MY STYLE *WORDS*:

_____
_____
_____
_____
_____
_____
_____

MY FAVE *PIECES*:

_____
_____
_____
_____
_____
_____
_____

MY *COLORS*:
_____
_____
_____
_____

MOODBOARD

sprinting through setbacks

GET UNAPOLOGETIC

We have to talk about being unapologetic with your style. What are things you've been told you 'shouldn't wear? Why?

I know that for me, I gave up wearing really bright colors for a while because all the 'serious athletes' wore mostly black. But that's not me! And similarly, I kept my hair really simple for a long time. But my braids are my favorite look—so now, I am unapologetic about them.

As women athletes, we also tend to feel like we 'shouldn't' care about our style or wear makeup or do our hair to train or compete. But I feel so much more powerful when my nails are done and my hair is looking great and I have on a bit of (waterproof) makeup. If doing any of that makes you feel more powerful, don't let anyone tell you that you can't!

List a few things that you've always wanted to wear but thought you couldn't or shouldn't. Then, plan a few outfits around them!

_____
_____
_____
_____
_____
_____
_____
_____
_____
_____

sprinting through setbacks

TAKE YOUR STYLE AND OWN IT

Now that you have a better sense of your personal style, it's time to figure out how it will work IRL.

How can you translate your style to casual, everyday life?
Let's be honest, none of us are dressing up every single day—we don't have time for that! But we can make sure everyday, we're adding a little bit of style to our usual uniform. What are little things you can add to everyday looks, like little pops of color or sneaky accessories that don't feel over-the-top (unless that's your vibe, in which case, love that for you!)

_____
_____
_____
_____
_____
_____

How can you pump it up for "race day"?
Take those style prompts and dial them up! (Again, you may have a few different outfits here for different big moments in your life.)

_____
_____
_____
_____
_____
_____
_____

OUTFIT
Planner

WEEK OF: _____

MONDAY

TOP:	
BOTTOM:	
SHOES:	
ACCESSORIES:	
OUTWEAR:	

TUESDAY

TOP:	
BOTTOM:	
SHOES:	
ACCESSORIES:	
OUTWEAR:	

WEDNESDAY

TOP:	
BOTTOM:	
SHOES:	
ACCESSORIES:	
OUTWEAR:	

THURSDAY

TOP:	
BOTTOM:	
SHOES:	
ACCESSORIES:	
OUTWEAR:	

FRIDAY

TOP:	
BOTTOM:	
SHOES:	
ACCESSORIES:	
OUTWEAR:	

What does the word joy bring to mind?

come back to your joy

sprinting through setbacks

GET READY FOR TOUGH TIMES

What are a couple of easy ways to make yourself feel instantly a little happier?
(I keep a few videos that make me happy on my phone.)

Who in your life can help shift your mood?
(For me, this is definitely my mom!)

How can you find ways to bring your light into situations?
(I remind myself to smile at the people around me, to try to make conversation and just lighten the mood a bit. I always want to contribute positive energy to any situation!)

Create a routine for when you aren't feeling good. How long do you let yourself have a pity party? How do you snap out of it?

sprinting through setbacks

START A GRATITUDE JOURNAL

You've probably heard of gratitude journals already, but they really do work! I try to use mine every day, and just write down a couple of things that I'm grateful for every single morning. Tiny things, big things—whatever feels right for you. It really helps keep things in perspective. Aim for at least three things you're grateful for. You can also think of them as highlights of the day if you don't like starting with "I'm thankful for...". Instead, just write out what your little and big wins from yesterday were! Still stuck? Add one thing you're looking forward to.

TODAY I'M GRATEFUL FOR
-
-
-
-

TODAY I'M GRATEFUL FOR
-
-
-
-

TODAY I'M GRATEFUL FOR
-
-
-
-

TODAY I'M GRATEFUL FOR
-
-
-
-

Gratitude Journal

TODAY I'M GRATEFUL FOR
- ....
- ....
- ....
- ....
- ....

TODAY I'M GRATEFUL FOR
- ....
- ....
- ....
- ....
- ....

TODAY I'M GRATEFUL FOR
- ....
- ....
- ....
- ....
- ....

TODAY I'M GRATEFUL FOR
- ....
- ....
- ....
- ....
- ....

TODAY I'M GRATEFUL FOR
- ....
- ....
- ....
- ....
- ....

TODAY I'M GRATEFUL FOR
- ....
- ....
- ....
- ....
- ....

sprinting through setbacks

WRITE OUT YOUR WHY

It's a lot easier to get through tough moments if you know *why* you're doing something. Having that written down is really helpful… and you can also use that Why Statement to make yourself some positive affirmations to say every day too! If your *Why* is that you want to be the best 400-meter runner that you can be, you can make an affirmation that says "I am a strong, fast runner." Stick that on your mirror so you see it first thing in the morning to keep your goals top of mind!

_____
_____
_____
_____
_____
_____
_____
_____
_____
_____
_____
_____
_____
_____

my WHY is...

sprinting through setbacks

REFRAME TOUGH MOMENTS

I feel like sometimes, bad things happen to you because something way better is around the corner. That's my way of accepting whatever is happening to me that might not be ideal—like getting food poisoning the day before a race! It feels like a more positive way to look at things, and usually it helps me move through those situations faster and with more grace. It's not always possible and it's not always easy, but when you can make it work for you, it can be a seriously helpful skill. In tough times, ask:

- How do I make this moment work for me?
- How can I make this situation better?
- What can I look forward to? (Even something really little!)

Try it here with something that didn't go your way recently: Ask these questions, and see how it changes your perspective!

_____
_____
_____
_____
_____
_____
_____
_____
_____
_____

sprinting through setbacks

THANKS FOR JOINING ME ON THIS JOURNEY!

I hope that these prompts helped you gain some inspiration, motivation, clarity, perspective and even some tips for navigating race day (and everyday!) with grace.

Thanks so much for taking this journey with me!

-Micha Powell

Get Your Copy of **SPRINTING THROUGH SETBACKS: AN OLYMPIAN'S GUIDE TO OVERCOMING SELF-DOUBT AND IMPOSTER SYNDROME** by Micha Powell at StrongGirlPublishing.com

www.ingramcontent.com/pod-product-compliance
Lightning Source LLC
Chambersburg PA
CBHW061154010526
44118CB00027B/2976